posh
· · · · · · ·

take care

ZEN COLORING

Teresa Roberts Logan

Andrews McMeel
PUBLISHING®

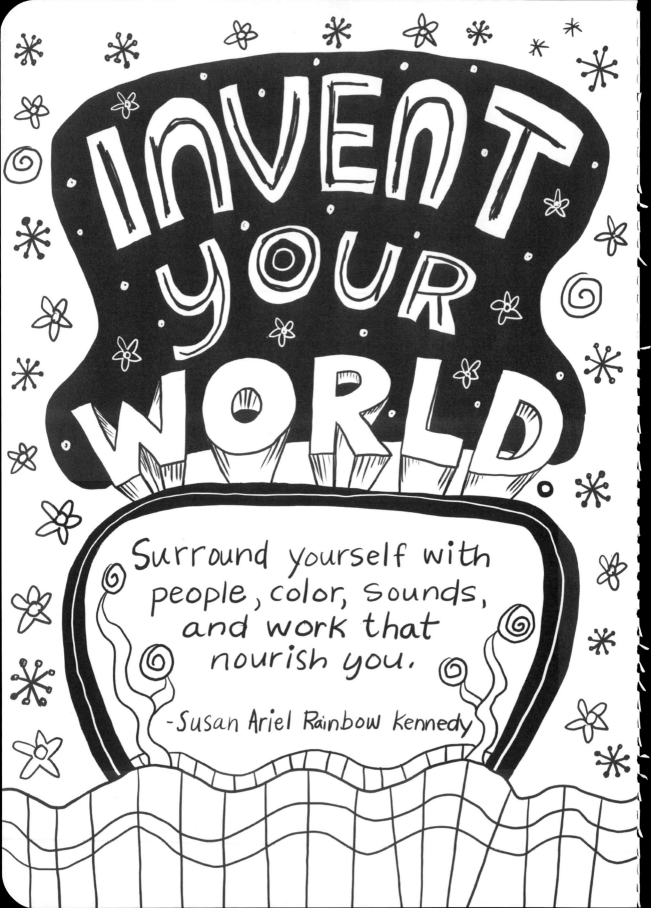

TELL ME, what is it you plan TO DO with your one WILD and precious Life? —MARY OLIVER

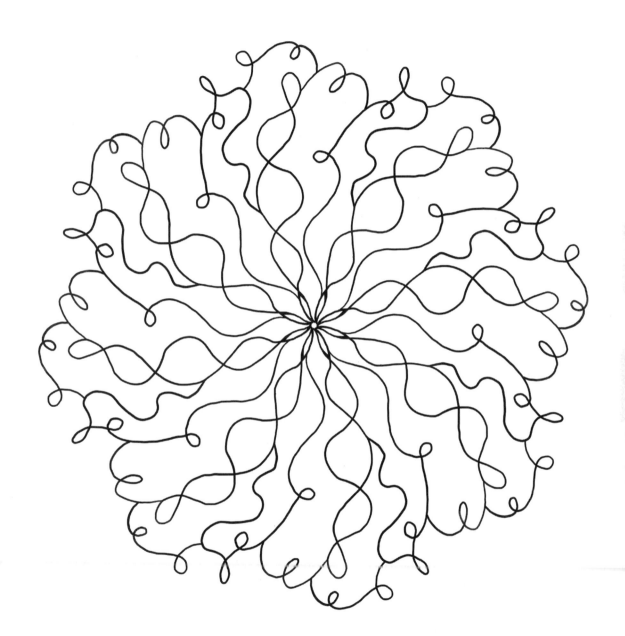

Just because you are happy does not mean that the day is perfect, but that you have looked beyond its imperfections.

— Bob Marley

Almost everything will work if you unplug it for a few minutes, including you.

—Anne Lamott

Instead of THINKING OUTSIDE THE BOX, GET RID of the BOX.

-DEEPAK CHOPRA

We delight in the beauty
of the butterfly, but rarely
ADMIT THE CHANGES
IT HAS GONE THROUGH
to achieve that beauty.

—MAYA ANGELOU

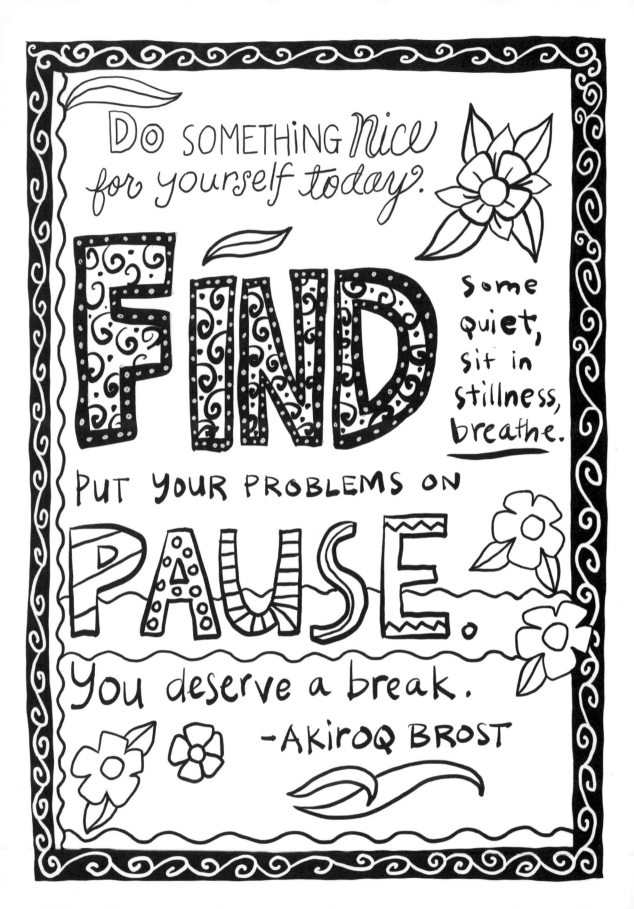

WHAT WE KNOW matters. WHO WE ARE MATTERS MORE.

—Brené Brown

Instructions for living a life:

Pay attention.

Be astonished.

Tell about it.

—mary oliver

ABOUT THE ARTIST

Teresa Roberts Logan is a cartoonist, comic, illustrator, and author based in Pittsburgh, Pennsylvania. She is the author of *Posh Coloring Book: Paisleys For Fun & Relaxation*, *Posh Coloring Book: Mandalas For Relaxation & Meditation*, and *The Older I Get, The Less I Care*, as well as the comics *The Bell Witch*, *Imagination*, *Zombies Alive*, *The Haunted Wing*, *The Ghost In The Buckaroo Basement*, *Haint Blue*, and *October*.

Known as the Laughing Redhead, she for years was a nationally touring stand-up comic, appearing on HBO, A&E, and The Comedy Channel.

She loves coloring, art making, travel, and drinking lots of hot tea.

www.LaughingRedhead.com
www.TeresaRobertsLogan.Art
Laughing Redhead Comics at GoComics.com
Twitter & IG: @LaughingRedhead

Andrews McMeel Publishing
a division of Andrews McMeel Universal
1130 Walnut Street, Kansas City, Missouri 64106

www.andrewsmcmeel.com

22 23 24 25 26 RLP 10 9 8 7 6 5 4 3 2 1

ISBN: 978-1-5248-7536-7

Editor: Allison Adler
Art Director: Julie Barnes
Production Editor: Jasmine Lim
Production Manager: Tamara Haus

ATTENTION: SCHOOLS AND BUSINESSES
Andrews McMeel books are available at quantity
discounts with bulk purchase for educational,
business, or sales promotional use. For information,
please e-mail the Andrews McMeel Publishing
Special Sales Department: specialsales@amuniversal.com.